Juliette Low

History Maker Bios

Susan Bivin Aller

LERNER PUBLICATIONS COMPANY • MINNEAPOLIS

Lerner Publications Company
A division of Lerner Publishing Group
241 First Avenue North
Minneapolis, MN 55401 U.S.A.

Website address: www.lernerbooks.com

Library of Congress Cataloging-in-Publication Data

Aller, Susan Bivin.
    Juliette Low / Susan Bivin Aller.
    p.   cm. — (History maker bios)
    Includes bibliographical references (p.   ) and index.
    ISBN-13: 978–0–8225–6580–2 (lib. bdg. : alk. paper)
    ISBN-10: 0–8225–6580–3 (lib. bdg. : alk. paper)
    1. Low, Juliette Gordon, 1860–1927—Juvenile literature. 2. Girl Scouts of the
United States of America—Biography—Juvenile literature. I. Title.
    HS3268.2.L68A44 2007
    369.463092—dc22 [B]   2006018976

Manufactured in the United States of America
1 2 3 4 5 6 – JR – 12 11 10 09 08 07

TABLE OF CONTENTS

INTRODUCTION

When her wealthy husband died, Juliette "Daisy" Gordon Low longed for something useful to do. One day, she met Sir Robert Baden-Powell. He had founded the Boy Scouts and its sister organization, the Girl Guides, in Great Britain. Daisy wanted to be part of this exciting new program.

Daisy started the first American Girl Guide troops in Savannah, Georgia, in 1912. The name was later changed to Girl Scouts of the USA. For the rest of her life, Daisy put everything she had into developing the Girl Scouts. For Daisy, Girl Scouting was a splendid game. No one had more fun playing it than she did.

This is her story.

1 "SHE'S A DAISY"

"**I** bet she's going to be a 'Daisy,'" her uncle said when she was born. "Daisy" was a name for something fine or first-rate. Her real name was Juliette Magill Kinzie Gordon. But her family called her Daisy from the start.

Daisy was the second child of William Washington Gordon II and Eleanor Kinzie Gordon. She was born in Savannah, Georgia, on October 31, 1860. Her father owned a cotton business. He came from an important southern family. People in Savannah admired him. His children did too. But they also played games with him and teased him.

HOME SWEET HOME

The beautiful house where Daisy's family lived in Savannah, Georgia, became the Juliette Gordon Low Girl Scout National Center. Called the Birthplace, it is open to the public. It is listed as a National Historic Landmark.

Daisy's mother came from Chicago, Illinois. Eleanor "Nellie" Kinzie had ancestors who fought in the Revolutionary War (1775–1783). Her grandfather built the first house in Chicago. Nellie loved being the center of attention. She danced and played the piano. She was stubborn and funny. She passed many of these traits to her daughter Daisy.

Daisy's mother, Eleanor Kinzie Gordon, in the 1860s

The United States began fighting the Civil War (1861–1865) after Daisy was born. The North fought the South over slavery. Daisy's father became an officer in the Confederate army of the South. Daisy's grandfather and uncles on her mother's side joined the Union army of the North. Daisy was too young to understand what the war was about. She knew only that her father went away to fight for weeks at a time. Daisy also knew her mother had a hard time getting enough food for her and her big sister, Eleanor, and the new baby, Alice.

Daisy's father, William Washington Gordon II, was an officer in the Confederate army.

When Daisy was four years old, a Union general named William T. Sherman marched his army through Georgia. He wanted to capture Savannah. Union soldiers invaded Savannah just before Christmas. They had more men and supplies than the Confederates. The people of Savannah had to surrender.

General Sherman (CENTER FRONT, ON RIGHT) talks with his soldiers near Atlanta, Georgia. They fought their way to Savannah in 1864.

Daisy at the age of four.

But General Sherman knew Nellie's relatives in Chicago. He paid a surprise visit to Nellie to make sure she was all right. One of Daisy's earliest memories was of sitting on General Sherman's knee. He gave her some rock candy. The war had made sugar very scarce. This was the first time she had ever tasted it.

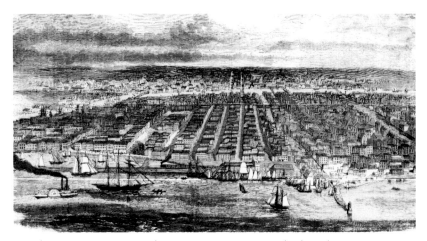

In the 1860s, more than 100,000 people lived in Chicago, Illinois.

After Savannah surrendered to the North, Daisy and her mother and sisters went to stay with her grandparents in Chicago. Daisy's father lost his cotton business. It would take a long time for him to rebuild it. Until then, he could not support his wife and children. Nellie sold some land she owned in Chicago. She sent the money to help her husband. Daisy was nearly five years old when her family reunited in Savannah after the war, in 1865. They moved back into the Gordon family home with her grandmother Gordon. Fortunately, it had not been damaged in the war.

Daisy was one of the brightest of the Gordon children. She had a lot of energy and curiosity. But she never could spell very well. Daisy said it was no use having a dictionary because she often didn't know what letter a word began with. She also mixed up words and said things that were funny without knowing it.

Daisy was ten years old when this photo was taken.

By the time Daisy was twelve, there were six Gordon children: Eleanor, Daisy, Alice, Bill, Mabel, and Arthur. Some summers, the Gordons and their cousins stayed with an aunt at Etowah Cliffs in northern Georgia. Their parents wanted to keep them safe from the yellow fever and malaria that struck during hot weather in Savannah. The children grew strong from outdoor exercise. Daisy's artistic talents blossomed. She wrote plays for her cousins to perform. She also painted, made paper dolls, and illustrated her own poems.

Clockwise from the front left, the six Gordons in this photo are Mabel, Eleanor, Daisy, Arthur, Bill, and Alice.

WARM MILK

Daisy was a tender-hearted child. She didn't want to see any person or animal suffer. She was always saving stray dogs and cats. One night, when the weather turned cold, she pinned together her mother's good blankets. Then she went to the barn and wrapped a cow in the blankets to keep it warm. By the next morning, the cow had stomped the blankets into the dirt.

Daisy liked organizing people for a good cause. She started a sewing club with her sisters and cousins. She called it the Helpful Hands club. They made clothes for the children of a poor family in town. But none of them really knew how to sew. The clothes fell apart the first time they were worn. One of the boys ripped his off in disgust and ran home naked. Daisy's family renamed the club the Helpless Hands.

2 AN INTERNATIONAL MARRIAGE

Wealthy southern families usually sent their children to private boarding schools. At age thirteen, Daisy began attending school in Virginia. From then on, she spent most of the year away at school. She became a talented sculptor and painter. She liked sports, especially horseback riding.

Daisy was an attractive young adult.

Daisy's warm nature made her very popular. Back in Savannah, she was considered one of the most charming young women in town.

Daisy's parents gave her a trip to Europe in 1882. In England, she went to visit friends of her parents, Mr. and Mrs. Andrew Low. The Lows owned grand homes in both England and Savannah. They were millionaires. Daisy and the Lows' daughters became good friends. The Lows had one son, William Mackay Low. People called him Willy. During her time with the family, Daisy and Willy fell in love.

They kept their love a secret for several years. Finally, they received their parents' permission to marry. As a wedding present, Willy's father planned to give the couple a house in Savannah. But a few months before the wedding, Willy's father died. Willy inherited the house and his father's business. He also received a huge fortune.

Daisy had her picture painted soon after she married Willy.

Daisy and Willy (CENTER) are surrounded by their attendants and family members in their wedding photo.

Daisy and Willy married in December 1886. As they left the church, friends threw a shower of rice to wish them well. A grain of rice lodged in Daisy's ear. A doctor tried to remove the rice, but he hurt her eardrum. A bad treatment for an earache had damaged her other ear the year before. Daisy became nearly deaf. In spite of her deafness, Daisy was as social as ever. It was easier for her to talk than to listen. People didn't realize that one reason she talked a lot was because she couldn't hear.

Daisy (THIRD FROM RIGHT) goes hunting in Scotland with Willy's friends from Britain. They enjoyed her company.

At first, the newlyweds lived in their Savannah home. But within one year, Willy convinced Daisy to move to Britain. Willy's friends adored Daisy. She attended their parties and sporting events. She became known for her dinner parties. She served fried chicken, ham, corn, and sweet potatoes from her father's farm in Georgia. Her guests had never tasted these American foods before.

Daisy and Willy were unable to have children. So Daisy gave her motherly care to her animals. She had a pet mockingbird, a parrot, and many dogs. She let the dogs sleep on her bed. She even painted portraits of them.

Daisy loved to ride horseback. But when she hurt herself in a riding accident, her doctor told her she should not ride again. Her deafness was getting worse. She had problems with her inner ear. This affected her balance.

This is Daisy's favorite photo of herself with a dog.

Daisy often stayed home while Willy went away with friends. While he was gone, he met another woman. He fell in love with her. He told Daisy he wanted a divorce. Daisy was crushed.

In 1905, Daisy heard more shocking news. Willy had died. He left most of his fortune to the other woman. He even left her the house in Savannah. Daisy hired lawyers. The lawyers fought to return Daisy's belongings to her.

1905 was a difficult year for Daisy.

Daisy felt sad and useless. She had no real work or duties. "I would like to get away from the world somewhere," she wrote to her mother, "and . . . start to do some work in life."

3 DAISY JOINS THE SCOUTS

Daisy's spirit and joy slowly returned. She bought a house in London and rented another in Scotland. She entertained friends and bought gifts for her nieces and nephews. She hunted deer with the young men and threw dinner parties for the girls.

Daisy depended on her family for support. Sometimes she asked her father to lend her money. Daisy had plenty of money. But she had trouble managing it because of her problems with arithmetic. She often thought somebody owed her money, when it was really the other way around. She filed her bills in four envelopes marked "This Year," "Next Year," "Some Time," and "Never."

DARING DAISY

During one of her stays in Savannah, Daisy bought a car. But she paid no attention to the rules of the road. One day, she crashed her car through a house. A family was having lunch there. Daisy backed the car out, found a phone, and called her brother. He asked her what she had said to the family. "Why, I didn't say anything," Daisy said. "I didn't think it would be polite to bother them while they were eating."

In 1910, at the age of fifty, Daisy traveled to Canada and Egypt. She toured Spain and France by car. She led an active life. But she still longed for something to give her life more purpose. In Paris, Daisy studied sculpting. She thought this might become her life's work. But after returning to London, she met the general and war hero Sir Robert Baden-Powell. She entertained him with stories of her studies in Paris. She discovered he was also a sculptor. They soon became friends.

Daisy created these sculptures of her father (LEFT) and her niece, Daisy Gordon (RIGHT).

Sir Robert Baden-Powell in 1910

Daisy and Robert had a lot in common. Robert had American ancestors. As a young man, he had studied the survival skills of American Indians. Daisy's ancestors had learned similar skills in the American wilderness. Robert taught his soldiers to use these skills. He called the men scouts.

Baden-Powell (CENTER FRONT) entertains a group of Boy Scouts camping out.

Robert Baden-Powell wrote a book called *Aids to Scouting.* Many young boys wrote to him and asked how they could become scouts. Robert responded by founding the Boy Scouts. By the time Daisy met Robert, there were forty thousand Boy Scouts in Britain, the United States, France, and Germany. Thousands of girls wanted to be scouts too. Robert's sister Agnes created a scouting club just for them. She called it the Girl Guides.

Daisy became interested in the Girl Guides. She liked the organization and its activities. Most of all, she saw a way to do something useful. In August 1911, Daisy organized her first Girl Guide group. She invited seven girls from poor families to her house in Scotland. She taught them skills in first aid and cooking. Then she showed them how they could earn money by raising chickens to sell the eggs. They also learned how to spin yarn from sheep's wool.

Daisy's Scottish Girl Guides owned sheep. She taught the girls to comb the sheep's wool, as the girl on the right is doing. Then they could spin the wool into yarn (LEFT, CENTER).

Daisy and Robert happened to be on the same ship sailing to the United States in 1912. Robert was touring the world to tell people about the Boy Scouts. On the ship, Daisy and Robert talked about starting Girl Guide groups in the United States. When Daisy arrived in Savannah, she phoned her cousin. "Come right over," she exclaimed. "I've got something for the girls of Savannah, and all America, and all the world, and we're going to start it tonight!"

4 THE SCOUTS COME TO THE UNITED STATES

Daisy didn't waste any time forming a Girl Guide troop in Savannah. She learned that her cousin's daughter went camping with a group of girls every Saturday. They studied with a nature expert in a nearby woods. They cooked supper over a campfire.

Daisy told the group that in Britain, Girl Guides wore uniforms. They camped and earned badges by learning skills. That sounded exciting to the American girls—especially the part about uniforms.

Daisy invited the girls to meet on March 12, 1912. She told them all about becoming Girl Guides. They recited the Guide Promise. They signed their names on a membership list. Daisy wrote the name of her niece and namesake, Daisy Gordon, on the top line. She wanted her favorite twelve-year-old to be the first Girl Guide in the United States.

Girl Guides from London raise a British flag at camp in France. Daisy's American girls wanted to wear uniforms too.

Daisy charmed her friends into helping with the Girl Guides. When someone tried to say no, she pretended she didn't hear her. Her friends usually gave in and became patrol leaders or board members. Daisy worked to help the Girl Guide movement grow. For more than four years, she used her own money to pay her staff and buy uniforms and handbooks.

The American Girl Guide movement grew quickly. In 1915, it changed its name to Girl Scouts of America. The leaders formed a national council. Daisy was its first president.

Daisy helped create the first Girl Scout handbook.

Girl Scouts pose with Daisy (BACK ROW, FOURTH FROM LEFT) in front of the Girl Scout Headquarters in Savannah.

By the next year, the Girl Scouts had seven thousand members. Soon paid staff members ran the national office. Daisy's friends volunteered and donated money. Many important women became honorary Girl Scouts. One was the wife of President Woodrow Wilson.

"Girl Scouting was a game to [Daisy], and she had the greatest fun playing it," one friend said. Daisy took troops on camping trips and taught them Robert Baden-Powell's scouting techniques. They studied nature and went boating and swimming. At night, Daisy entertained them around the campfire. She told ghost stories and tales from the American frontier. The girls' favorite story was about Daisy's great-grandmother. She had been captured by Native Americans.

STRONG WOMEN

Daisy came from a long line of pioneer women. They lived through wars and other scary experiences. Seneca Indians captured her great-grandmother. They kept her for four years before letting her go. Daisy's grandmother slept with two pistols to protect her family from danger on the frontier.

In Daisy's time, people thought most sports were unladylike. But Girl Scouting encouraged girls to play sports. Daisy had a basketball court made for her Girl Scouts. She had them wear loose blouses over pants called bloomers. Girls back then wore dresses or skirts. They weren't supposed to wear pants. Daisy hung curtains to hide the court from the street.

These girls are wearing bloomers to play basketball, as Daisy's Girl Scouts did.

Some Girl Scouts collected peach pits during World War I (1914–1918). The pits were ground up to use in gas masks. The masks protected soldiers from harmful chemicals used in the war.

You Save Peach Seeds — They Will Save Soldiers ►Lives◄

When the United States entered World War I in 1917, the Girl Scouts did important work. They sewed clothes for soldiers and served food to servicemen. They helped nurses when thousands of people fell ill with the flu. Girl Scouts also planted vegetable gardens. They wanted to make sure Americans had enough to eat. Many girls helped the war effort by joining Girl Scout troops.

As president of the Girl Scouts, Daisy traveled widely. She talked about the organization and raised money for it. She loved her uniform and wore it everywhere. She liked the stiff, wide-brimmed hat and the sturdy Girl Scout shoes. She wore a special belt that held a scout knife, a whistle, and a tin drinking cup. She once stood on her head at a board meeting to show off her new uniform shoes.

With the Girl Scouts, Daisy finally found her life's work. She found something else too—the daughters she never had.

Daisy (CIRCLED) is surrounded by members of her Girl Scout family.

5 CIRCLING THE GLOBE

Daisy often traveled to Britain. She built cooperation between the British Girl Guides and the American Girl Scouts. One year, she crossed the Atlantic Ocean seven times. She even sailed during World War I. Sailing was dangerous then. Enemy submarines threatened ships.

After the war ended, Daisy represented the United States at the first International Council of Girl Guides and Girl Scouts. It took place in London in 1919. Daisy proudly reported that American Girl Scouts numbered forty thousand.

Daisy focused on the girls who made up the organization. "The girls must always come first," she told the leaders. "The girls will decide whether the plan is good or not. . . . You can trust them to know." Daisy wrote letters to the troops she started in Savannah. She also visited Girl Scout camps wherever she went. She joined in campfire cookouts and hikes. She pretended to read palms. The "fortunes" she told were really wise advice.

Daisy (FAR LEFT) loved to visit her Girl Scouts.

Daisy was world famous. But the girls cherished her as a friend. They called her Miss Daisy.

The Girl Scout Law tells girls to "make the world a better place." Daisy wanted the Girl Scouts to have groups in every country. She believed they could link nations together in friendship. She dreamed of holding another international meeting of Girl Guides and Girl Scouts. But this time, she wanted the World Camp to be in the United States. By 1925, Daisy was in a hurry to realize her dream. She didn't have much time. She was suffering from an incurable cancer.

In the spring of 1926, five hundred Girl Guide and Girl Scout members from thirty countries came together at Camp Edith Macy in Westchester County, New York. Daisy's Girl Scout work had reached its highest point. She had indeed given scouting to the girls of the whole world.

Girl Guides and Girl Scouts from thirty countries met at the 1926 World Camp in New York State.

Daisy went to Britain to see friends one last time. Then she returned to Savannah. Daisy hoped she would not need her family to care for her. She wanted never to become old and boring. She never did. In spite of her pain, she stayed active until the end. She died in Savannah on January 17, 1927. She was sixty-six years old. Before she died, Daisy added a sentence to her will. She wanted to leave her most valued things to her family. These things were her friendships—"especially my beloved Girl Scouts."

TIMELINE

In the year . . .

1865   the North defeated the South in the Civil War.
Daisy, her mother, and her sisters spent part of the year in Chicago. Then they returned to Savannah.

1874   Daisy left home to attend boarding school in Virginia.   `Age 13`

1882   she toured Europe and visited the Low family in Britain.

1885   a bad treatment for an earache damaged her hearing in one ear.

1886   she married William Mackay (Willy) Low. a doctor ruined her other eardrum during an operation. She became nearly deaf.   `Age 26`

1887   she moved with Willy to Britain.

1905   Willy died.   `Age 44`

1911   she met Sir Robert Baden-Powell. she formed a Girl Guide patrol in Scotland.

1912   she returned to Savannah, Georgia. she organized the first Girl Guide patrol in the United States.   `Age 51`

1915   she became the first president of the newly named Girl Scouts of America.

1919   she attended the first International Council of Girl Guides and Girl Scouts in London.

1926   she organized and led the World Camp at Camp Edith Macy in New York.

1927   she died in Savannah on January 17.   `Age 66`

HONORING THE FOUNDER

The Girl Scouts call Juliette Gordon Low the Founder. To remember her, they celebrate Founder's Day every year on her birthday. Schools, camps, and even a ship—the S.S. *Juliette Low*—have been named for her. A U.S. postage stamp featured her picture in 1948. In 1979, she became a member of the National Women's Hall of Fame.

But the Girl Scouts of the USA is her greatest memorial. It is the largest educational organization for girls in the world. It has a membership of nearly four million girls and women. Charming, fun-loving Daisy Low would be proud of her "beloved Girl Scouts."

The S.S. JULIETTE LOW was launched from Savannah on May 12, 1944.

FURTHER READING

Brown, Fern G. *Daisy and the Girl Scouts: The Story of Juliette Gordon Low.* Morton Grove, IL: Albert Whitman, 1996. Featuring black-and-white illustrations and photos, this book tells the story of Juliette Low.

Eubanks, Toni. *Octavia's Girl Scout Journey: Savannah 1916.* New York: Girl Scouts of the USA, 1999. This illustrated historical novel tells the adventures of a Savannah Girl Scout in 1916.

Girl Scouts of the USA. *Junior Girl Scout Handbook.* New York: Girl Scouts of the USA, 2001. The official handbook includes ideas for activities and service projects.

Kent, Deborah. *Juliette Gordon Low: Founder of the Girl Scouts of America.* Chanhassen, MN: Child's World, 2003. This brief biography includes large photos, some in color.

WEBSITES

Juliette Gordon Low Birthplace
http://www.girlscouts.org/birthplace The website of the
Birthplace includes facts, pictures, and information for
visitors.

National Women's Hall of Fame: Juliette Gordon Low
http://www.greatwomen.org/women.php?action=viewone
&id=100 This website outlines the life of Juliette Gordon
Low, who was elected to this group in 1979.

Official Website of the Girl Scouts of the USA
http://www.girlscouts.org/ This website gives information
about the history of the Girl Scouts, the life of Juliette
Gordon Low, and the programs of the Girl Scouts.

SELECT BIBLIOGRAPHY

Choate, Anne Hyde, and Helen Ferris, eds. *Juliette Low
and the Girl Scouts.* Whitefish, MT: Kessinger
Publishing, 2003. First published 1928 by Girl Scouts,
Inc.

Pace, Mildred Mastin. *Juliette Low.* Ashland, KY: Jesse
Stuart Foundation, 1997.

Shultz, Gladys Denny, and Daisy Gordon Lawrence. *Lady
from Savannah: the Life of Juliette Low.* Philadelphia:
J. B. Lippincott Co., 1958.

INDEX

Acknowledgments

For photographs and artwork: Collection of the Juliette Gordon Low Birthplace, Girl Scout National Center, Savannah, GA, pp. 4, 7, 8, 9, 11, 13, 14, 17, 19, 20, 21, 22, 26 (both), 33, 34, 38, 40, 42, 45; Library of Congress, pp. 10 (LC-B811-3626), 36 (LC-USZ62-71237); © North Wind Picture Archives, p. 12; © National Portrait Gallery, Smithsonian Institution/Art Resource, NY, p. 18; © Rischgitz/Getty Images, p. 27; © Topical Press Agency/Getty Images, p. 28; © Hulton Archive/Getty Images, p. 29; © Hulton-Deutsch Collection/CORBIS, p. 30; © Bettmann/CORBIS, p. 37. **Front and Back Cover:** Collection of the Juliette Gordon Low Birthplace, Girl Scout National Center, Savannah, GA. **For quoted material:** pp. 6, 23, 26, 40, 43, Gladys Denny Shultz and Daisy Gordon Lawrence, *Lady from Savannah: the Life of Juliette Low* (Philadelphia: J. B. Lippincott Co., 1958); pp. 30, 35, Anne Hyde Choate and Helen Ferris, eds., *Juliette Low and the Girl Scouts* (1928; repr., Whitefish, MT: Kessinger Publishing, 2003); p. 41, Girl Scouts of the USA website, http://www.girlscouts.org/program/gs_central/promise_law/.